Contents

The home front

For British people the Second World War was a 'people's war'. Everyone took part — from the youngest to the oldest, from those who went off to fight to those who stayed behind on the 'home front'.

War began in 1939. After German troops invaded Poland, Britain and France declared war on Germany. The war lasted six years and, by the time it ended in 1945, nearly every country in the world was involved. It was different from previous wars. Huge numbers of civilians — ordinary men and women — were caught up in war just as much as soldiers, sailors and other armed forces. Air raids, food rationing, evacuation and the threat of invasion brought war directly into people's daily lives and meant that everyone was affected.

It's war!

On 1 September 1939 newspaper headlines announced that Nazi Germany had invaded Poland. Two days later Britain and its empire and France declared war on Germany. The Second World War had begun.

Taking part

For the British people it was like being on a war front, even if they were living at home. Everyone had a job to do, whether it was saving water, food and scrap metal, defending the country from possible invasion, working in wartime industries, or helping the wounded and homeless.

All change

Britain in 1939 was very different from today. Mobile phones and the Internet did not exist. Very few families owned their own homes. Poverty was widespread. Many homes had outside toilets and only cold-water taps. Most people did not travel abroad. Women worked but only in jobs thought suitable for them. Six years of war brought great changes.

WOMEN OF BRITAIN

COME INTO THE FACTORIES

ASK AT ANY EMPLOYMENT EXCHANGE FOR ADVICE AND FULL DETAILS

Women needed

As men went off to fight, posters called for women volunteers to fill vacant jobs. Posters like this one appealed for women to do factory work.

66 The whole of the warring nations are engaged, not only soldiers but the entire population, men, women and children. The fronts are everywhere.99

Winston Churchill, Prime Minister, 20 August 1940

Being prepared

As war came closer, the government started preparing. People dug shelters, put on gas masks and got ready.

Many British people did not want a war. Older people had lived through the First World War (1914–18) and most had lost relatives. When war came again feelings varied: young people were excited or scared. Older people were often resigned or sad.

Lights off

Most people thought that Germany would drop bombs on Britain immediately. Poison gas had been used in the trenches during the First World War, so everyone was given a gas mask. They were uncomfortable and smelly.

Causing confusion

Workmen took down signposts so that if German troops invaded they would not know where they were. British people often got confused as well.

"It was Sunday morning... we heard war had been declared... I was cycling home and there was this very officious ARP [Air Raid Precautions] man blowing his whistle, 'Get under cover!' So I was pedalling like mad to get home and everyone was very apprehensive..."

Peter Smith, schoolboy, Kent

At night streetlights were switched off. Torches and vehicle headlamps had special covers. Families made thick blackout curtains to cover windows so no light could escape. Air-raid wardens walked around telling people to 'switch off that light'. Everyone had to carry an identity (ID) card and local councils organised for air-raid shelters to be built. Some people were issued with, or bought, their own shelters and put them up in their garden or inside their home.

Phoney war

Air-raid sirens sounded the day war was declared. Some people rushed into shelters or just waited. But bombing did not start. In Britain, very little happened for the first few months after war was declared. People called that time the 'phoney war' because everyone was prepared but there was no sign of the enemy. Fighting was taking place elsewhere however, particularly in France after May 1940, and from September 1940, heavy air raids started.

Blue in the face, 1940

A nurse puts a baby into a special gas mask as part of a routine practice. Teenager Dorothy Williams said her baby sister, "... screamed the place down and went quite blue in the face", when she was put into hers.

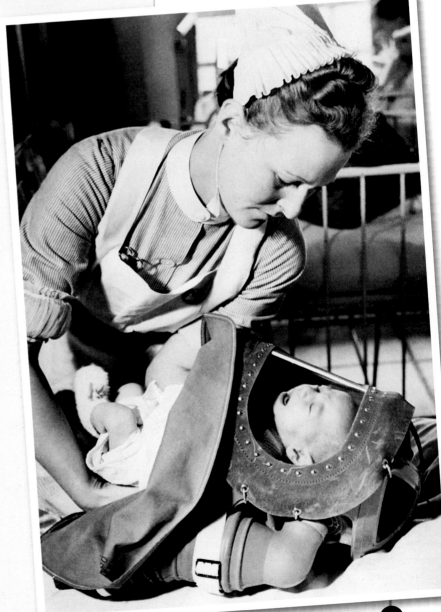

Moving to safety

Many British children were evacuated from cities and towns to escape air raids. Most were sent into the countryside for safety, often to live with complete strangers.

Hundreds of thousands of children were sent away from their homes during the war. They included babies, toddlers and school-age children. The youngest travelled with their mothers; others had to leave parents behind. For some children, evacuation was a great adventure but for others it was bewildering.

Into the unknown

Children usually did not know where they were going. They lined up, often in playgrounds, and marched to the nearest station. They wore name labels, carried a bag, gas mask and often a favourite toy.

When they reached their destination, children were billeted, or housed, with foster families. Often they waited while people chose the children they wanted. It was embarrassing and upsetting.

Leaving home, 1940

Clutching his suitcase with both hands, this young boy leaves London with a group of other evacuees.

> "Helen started to cry when she saw my mother, and asked, 'Mum, why can't we come home?'"
>
> *Gwendoline Stewart, schoolgirl*

A new life

Two London evacuees feed pigs in Wales. Many Londoners had never seen pigs or cows before the war. They enjoyed helping farmers.

Like a parcel

These evacuees have left Bristol and are arriving in Devon. Some evacuees said they felt like parcels because they had luggage labels showing their name, age and address pinned to their coats.

New experiences

Most host families were welcoming and made evacuees comfortable. Some were not kind and did not treat children well. Country life was strange for inner-city children who had never seen fields or cows before. Host families were often shocked by the poverty of inner-city children and could not understand them.

> "... we had to walk up the road past some cows behind a fence in a field. I was terrified... I had never seen a cow before, only the pictures, and to me the cows were very big and the fence so small..."
>
> *Leslie Alexander, schoolboy evacuee*

Defending the home front

In 1940 there were fears that Germany would invade Britain. A 'Home Guard' formed to defend villages, towns and coastal areas from invasion.

When war broke out, men volunteered or were called up to go off and fight. Some stayed behind because they were working in 'reserved' occupations such as farming or engineering, and were needed on the home front. Others were too old or young to go and fight. In May 1940 the British government appealed to these men to do their bit to defend the country.

Dad's Army, 1940

When the Home Guard was first formed, they did not have proper uniforms or even guns. They drilled with brooms and sticks, which they would have used to defend the country.

> "My father was in the Home Guard. One day he was showing us how to present arms, not with his rifle but with a music stand, and he shot it through the window and broke the glass..."

Peter Bennett, schoolboy, Surrey

'Dad's Army'

About a million and a half men came forward. Some had been soldiers in the First World War but others had not done any military training. Because many of them were quite elderly, they were often jokingly known as 'Dad's Army'.

At first the Home Guard had very little proper equipment. Even so, they trained and drilled and learned to use firearms. They were a common sight in every village and town throughout Britain. Many prepared to defend coastal towns such as Folkestone or Dover, which is where an invasion was expected. Eventually the threat of invasion passed but the Home Guard did other duties, such as mine clearance, and manned anti-aircraft guns. They were finally stood down in December 1944.

Standing easy

People made jokes about the Home Guard, but they were a dedicated military defence force in the early months of the war. No one doubted their courage.

> "The army... dug huge trenches and took poles from the trees [and] stood these up at an angle and put camouflage netting over... and that did look as if there was a whole line of guns through the woods to deceive the enemy... we went to play in it... it was the silliest place to play..."

John Hammon, schoolboy, Kent

The Blitz

Air raids began in September 1939. From September 1940 London and other British cities experienced nightly bombing raids, known as the Blitz. Thousands of civilians were killed or made homeless.

Every night wailing air-raid sirens warned that German bomber aircraft were on their way. Air-raid wardens and police pounded the streets, urging people to take shelter. As high-explosive bombs rained down, the noise was terrible and buildings shook.

The Blitz spirit

People managed to have fun in air-raid shelters. They took their knitting and listened to music. Some shelters even had pianos.

"We used to sleep on the platform at Lambeth North Station. We'd go down in our pyjamas with a blanket and we'd take sandwiches and a flask. We stayed down there all night... came up at dawn and walked home..."

George Frankland, Londoner

Sheltering underground, 1940

Rich and poor slept side by side in the Underground during the Blitz. There were chemical toilets. It sometimes got smelly but people were friendly and felt safe.

There were public air-raid shelters but they could not hold everyone. Thousands of Londoners made their way to the Underground. There they spent the night packed like sardines on platforms or escalators. Some families retreated to Anderson shelters, corrugated iron structures, in their garden. Others preferred to stay in their homes. They huddled under the stairs, in cellars or, from February 1941, in steel-framed Morrison shelters.

> **"**My father rushed in and threw my mother and me underneath the kitchen table, and we heard an almighty explosion. It was a landmine on a parachute. It landed in the next road and killed several families.**"**
>
> *Eric Hill, schoolboy, Southampton*

A way of life

The air raids were frightening and they disrupted normal living. But as time went on, people on the home front got into a routine. Every evening after tea, they grabbed blankets and other possessions and made their way to the nearest shelter for the night. They only came out when the 'all clear' sounded.

The Blitz ended in May 1941. More than 40,000 civilians had been killed across Britain. Many children were orphaned. One in ten of the dead were children under the age of 16.

Brave dog

This reconstruction of an actual event shows an air-raid warden and his dog searching the rubble of a bombed-out building looking for survivors. The dog, Rip, was given a medal for bravery.

Helping others

War brought devastation to the home front. Air raids destroyed streets, houses and public buildings. Ordinary people volunteered help, often working in dangerous conditions.

Making good, 1944

Men of the Blitz repair squad take a welcome break and accept a cup of cocoa from a woman whose home has been bombed. Builders from all over Britain volunteered to repair bomb damage.

Civilians worked as auxiliary firefighters, working tirelessly to bring fires under control. Others worked as bomb disposal officers, defusing unexploded bombs in the streets. Many volunteered to be air-raid wardens, helping people into shelters and digging through rubble to save people's lives. Some teenagers helped the air-raid wardens, taking messages and even putting out incendiary bombs.

"At dawn we used to wait while they were pulling people out of wrecked places. There were people wandering around in their nightshifts... blood streaming down their faces. We tried to comfort them as best we could."

Marguerite Crowther, ambulance driver, London

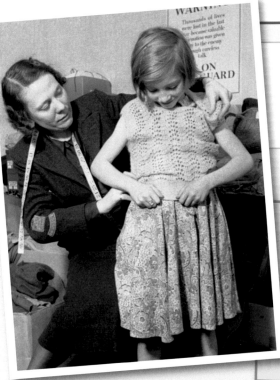

A new jumper

A member of the WVS helps a young girl try on a jumper. The girl's home and clothes were destroyed in an air raid.

"... it [an incendiary bomb] went off in my face and blew me straight back. I remember going past everybody about two feet off the ground and slamming against the wall..."

Peter Izard, teenager, civil defence messenger

Helping the homeless

Many people joined voluntary organisations such as the Women's Voluntary Service (WVS). These women handed out blankets and cups of tea to bombed-out families. They set up clothing exchanges and helped to re-house civilians who had been left homeless.

Churches and community centres became food and clothing centres. Ambulance drivers and Red Cross nurses treated the wounded and got them to hospital.

Tea and sympathy

A policeman hands a cup of tea to a man left homeless by a V1 flying bomb attack. The man's wife was killed in this incident.

Rationing

Today we buy food whenever we want and as much as we can afford. During the war food was rationed. People could only buy fixed amounts — and they had to make them last.

Britain had imported most of its food before the war. Once war began — particularly at sea — it was difficult to get food from abroad. The government set up a Ministry of Food to organise supplies and introduced rationing so food could be shared out equally.

Food for a week, 1942

This tray contains a ration book and one week's rations of sugar, tea, margarine, lard, eggs, bacon and cheese for one adult. Very few people had fridges so hoarding was difficult.

Unusual foods

Imported foods such as bananas and oranges disappeared from the shops, and basic items such as meat, eggs, butter, cheese and sugar were all strictly rationed. Root vegetables were not rationed so the government gave advice on using crops, such as carrots and turnips. A cartoon character called 'Potato Pete' promoted potatoes, which were filling and nutritious. Women, who did most of the cooking then, experimented with recipes. They used carrots to sweeten cakes,

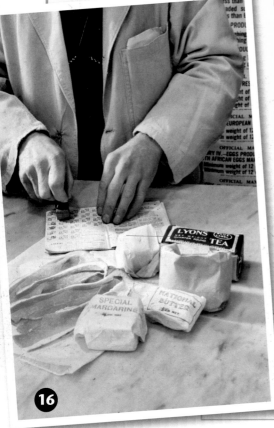

Local shop

A shopkeeper stamps a ration book. Everyone had a ration book. People shopped at their local grocer and butcher shops as there were no supermarkets.

and dried eggs and milk powder to make rather rubbery omelettes. Whale meat steaks were available and butchers sometimes sold horsemeat, which was stringy. Bread was not rationed but the wartime loaf was grey and dusty. Another wartime recipe was Woolton Pie, made from oats and root vegetables.

Staying healthy

Sweets were also rationed. One week's ration was equal to a very small chocolate bar. Children were given extra milk and cod-liver oil for health. People could buy food and luxury goods on the 'black market' but it was illegal. Food was also available through school dinners and works canteens. Most people on the home front learned to live with shortages, and actually ate more healthily than today.

Saving water

During wartime you could not have a bath more than 12 cm deep. This man shows where the water level should be — not a very deep bath at all.

> **"My sister didn't know what a banana was until after the war…"**
>
> *Joan Reed, schoolgirl, Essex*

Stand in line

People spent hours queuing for food on the home front. Queues formed whenever word went round that a shop was selling eggs or meat.

Digging for victory

The British government urged civilians to increase their food supply by growing fruit and vegetables. Adults and children began to 'dig for victory'.

As far as food went, country people were better off during the war than those in towns or cities. They grew their own vegetables and could catch rabbits or pheasants for extra meat. In autumn, they gathered hips and berries from hedgerows to make into syrups, jams or homemade wine. Town people relied on shops, but as war continued many started growing their own food.

> "I went in for a fancy dress competition… I dressed up as a gardener and put some vegetables in my little wheelbarrow and wore an apron and an old straw hat and I had 'Dig for Victory' on the side of the wheelbarrow. I got first prize…"
>
> *Peter Bennett, schoolboy, Surrey*

School dinners, 1943

These boys are picking vegetables, which they have grown at school. The vegetables will be cooked for their school dinners.

Land girls

Thousands of civilian women volunteered to work on the land during the war as members of the Women's Land Army (WLA), or 'land girls'. As men left farms to go and fight, women took over their jobs. Most land girls had never worked on a farm. They started early in the morning and laboured in the fields until early evening. They worked in all weathers and conditions. By 1943 land girls were producing about 70 per cent of the nation's food.

Allotments for all

The government also started a 'Dig for Victory' campaign. Every available piece of land was turned over to allotments, where town people could grow their own vegetables and fruit. Allotments were built in all public spaces, including parks and football grounds. After the Blitz, even bombsites were cleared and used for growing food. Civilians also grew produce in their gardens. Some kept pigs, rabbits or chickens for meat and eggs.

> **"** ... in the middle of winter... we used to have to wash the mud off the potatoes in cold water... it was unbearably cold...**"**
>
> *Vera Holdstock, land girl, Penhill Farm, Kent*

Going green

Boys clear rubble from a London bombsite so they can grow green beans. Growing vegetables helped the war effort because it meant ships could carry troops and equipment rather than food supplies.

Making do

Many basic household items were scarce during the war. Clothes were rationed, and people were encouraged to 'make do and mend'.

Clothes rationing began in June 1941. You couldn't go out and buy new clothes whenever you wanted. Everyone was allowed a certain number of points and could only buy clothes worth that number. To save material, clothes were made according to strict government regulations, without frills. Wartime furniture was also basic.

War on waste

Householders sorted every item of household waste. Old pots and pans and tin cans were salvaged to make aircraft. In fact much of the scrap was unsuitable but people felt they were doing their bit.

A stitch in time

Instead of buying new clothes, people made do with what they had. They mended clothes to make them last or altered them to make new outfits.

Recycled elephant, 1943

New toys were scarce. This much-loved elephant was made from scraps of material, stuffed with cotton and old stockings.

Women managed to make clothes from bedcovers, sheets, curtains and blankets. They used parachute silk, which was beautifully smooth. Make-up and stockings were scarce, so women reddened their lips with beetroot juice, and rubbed shoe polish or gravy browning on their legs to look like stockings.

Recycling experts

All sorts of everyday items were in short supply. People walked or cycled instead of using cars. Families re-used paper bags and cut up newspapers for lavatory paper. People thought it was wrong to waste anything. They felt that everything saved helped the war effort.

> **"**I had a wonderful surprise one Christmas... my parents wheeled a dolls' pram in... [it] was made by my father... of wood, all lacquered black... my mother had difficulty in getting a doll... she met a lady in a bus queue who said, 'I've got one at home.' That's how I got my doll...**"**
>
> *Pamela Leopard, Kent*

Cheerful savers

War is expensive. These village children have contributed to the National Savings Scheme to raise money for aeroplanes and weapons. The chart shows how much money their village has saved.

Working lives

During the war, factories switched from peacetime production to making weapons. Thousands of women entered the workforce.

When war broke out many men went off to fight. Women took over their jobs. They worked as bus conductors and postal workers. They trained as welders and engineers and made weapons. Many did jobs that only men had done before.

A heavy workload

Some people thought it was wrong for women to do the same work as men. Trade unions worried men would not get 'their' jobs back. But more men were called up and in December 1941 the government began conscripting women. Women did not get the same wages as men but people recognised their importance.

> **"**On night duty we would have to put the beds into the centre of the ward to prevent flying glass from coming in from falling bombs...**"**
>
> *Evelyn White, nurse, London*

Tickets please

Before the war women bus conductors were very unusual. But as men left to fight, women took over all their jobs.

Bevin Boys

Coal was needed urgently. Young men aged 18 to 25 were conscripted to work in the mines. They were called Bevin Boys after Ernest Bevin, Minister for Labour.

Women with children had a heavy workload. With husbands away, women combined long hours in factories and offices with childcare and looking after the home. For most women the war years were exhausting. Young people started work earlier than now as well. During the war, more than 70 per cent of boys and girls aged 14 to 17 went into full-time work.

Keeping going

Despite air raids and blackouts, civilians tried to carry on working as normal. Even after heavy bombing raids, shopkeepers, office workers and bank clerks set off to work. Doctors and nurses worked through air raids. Schools continued but lessons were often cut short so some children received little schooling.

Doing his bit, 1941

Workers arrived in Britain from the West Indies. They were British citizens and wanted to help with war work. This man is helping to make tanks.

> **"**... you had to get to work... I had to walk through the city centre of Birmingham... going round craters, stepping over hosepipes... even if you arrived at the office at eleven o'clock they were still pleased to see you because everybody was making the same effort...**"**
>
> *Gwendoline Stewart*

New faces

Today, Britain is a multicultural society, but in the 1940s it was not. The arrival of troops from all over the world brought new faces onto the home front.

As early as 1939 foreign troops were arriving in Britain to take part in the war against Nazi Germany. Some came from Canada, India and the West Indies, all of which were part of what was then the British Empire. Others included French, Poles, Czechs, Dutch and Belgians. Their countries had been occupied by Germany and they wanted to carry on fighting from Britain.

Americans arrive

In 1941 the United States entered the war on Britain's side. By 1944 some 1.5 million American personnel were stationed in Britain. Relations between Americans and British people were rather strained at first. Americans were far better fed than the British and not suffering shortages. They were shocked by the drab greyness and austerity of Britain. Many British thought Americans were brash, casual and noisy. Some American troops were black. Most British people had not seen black Americans before.

Over here

Black people were rare in Britain before the war, and black US soldiers virtually unknown. The US army segregated black and white soldiers, but most British people saw them as equal.

> **"**Canadians… were very, very friendly towards us… we had chocolate bars, tins of fruit, boxes of cheese… given to us by these visiting troops…**"**
>
> *Dennis Hayden, schoolboy, Hampshire*

The Americans fascinated British children and teenagers. They seemed glamorous, easy-going and looked as if they had come out of the movies. Young British women dated American GIs and American foods, dances and expressions entered the British way of life.

Seeing the sights, 1942

Two Polish airmen stroll around Piccadilly Circus in London. White stripes have been painted on the column behind them so cars do not drive into it during the blackout.

Seeking safety

Between 1938 and 1940 some 10,000 Jewish children arrived in Britain from Germany on what was called the Kindertransport (children's transport). They were fleeing Nazi persecution and were fostered with British families. Most never saw their parents again because they died in concentration camps. Also in Britain were Italian and German prisoners of war (POWs). Some helped the British war effort, working on farms.

Freedom

A Russian soldier strums a home-made balalaika in a military camp in Sussex. He had been a prisoner of war of the Germans but escaped to freedom in Britain.

This is the news

Radio — or wireless as it was called then — was a lifeline for people on the home front. Civilians listened to the radio for news, advice and fun.

When Britain declared war in 1939 people heard the news on the radio, at 11.15 am on 3 September 1939. From then on, families gathered round the radio every evening to hear the latest news bulletins. War correspondents broadcast vivid accounts of air and naval battles. Schoolchildren charted events on maps, using small paper flags. During the most difficult times, wartime leader Winston Churchill broadcast stirring speeches to raise morale.

Advice and comedy

The government used the BBC (British Broadcasting Corporation) to give advice on rationing, or to encourage civilians to take part in campaigns such as 'Make Do and Mend'. There were also music programmes featuring popular songs of the day, and classical music.

Millions of children tuned in to the radio at 5 pm every evening to listen to Children's Hour,

Taking a break
Munitions workers drink a welcome cuppa, share a joke and listen to the radio during a much-needed break from work. The BBC broadcast special programmes for workers, such as 'Music While You Work', which played in factories.

presented by 'Uncle Mac'. Radio also made people laugh. One popular radio show was 'It's That Man Again', featuring characters such as 'Mrs Mopp' and 'Funf', a comic German spy.

Having fun

Despite the hardships of war, people enjoyed themselves. Adults and children flocked to the cinema every week, even staying in their seats when the air-raid sirens sounded. They watched adventure films, romances and cartoons, forgetting about war for a while.

Entertainers such as singer Vera Lynn and American big bands also took part in the war effort, providing concerts and shows on the home front. Dances were popular too. And at home people played the piano and sang.

It's that man, 1944

ITMA — 'It's That Man Again' — featured Tommy Handley, shown here rehearsing with other actors. Catch phrases from the show entered the language.

War ends

The Second World War finally ended in 1945. On the home front lights came back on and church bells rang out. People celebrated but it would take time to adjust to peace.

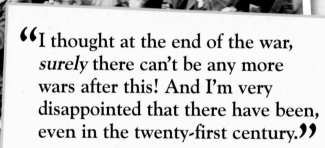

> **"I thought at the end of the war,** *surely* **there can't be any more wars after this! And I'm very disappointed that there have been, even in the twenty-first century."**
>
> *John Tatum*

Deadliest war

For six years people on the home front had lived with war on a daily basis. It had been the deadliest war in history. In Britain, more than 60,000 civilians had been killed. More than 7,000 were children. Many more had been injured. Thousands of homes had been destroyed. People now had to overcome the damage of the war years and take part in rebuilding for peace.

> **"** ...We went out in the garden with all our neighbours. We lit a huge bonfire... Everybody made wine: dandelion, rhubarb, mangel... We had a wonderful celebration...**"**
>
> *Noel Dumbrell, schoolboy, Sussex*

Singing for joy, 1945

Servicemen and women link arms and sing as they walk through Piccadilly Circus in London. It is August 1945 and Japan has surrendered, finally bringing an end to six years of war.

Difficult adjustments

When war ended, soldiers began returning home. For many families it was not always easy to adjust. Children had not seen fathers for many years. Women had coped on their own, working and bringing up children. Now women had to give up work and go back into the home again. Husbands and fathers were welcomed back but in the early years, families often felt like strangers to each other. And there were families where men never returned because they had been killed fighting abroad.

Overcoming shortages

Shortages continued for many years. Food rationing lasted until 1954. New homes were desperately needed. Slowly, however, conditions began to improve. In 1945 there was an election. The new Labour government introduced a National Health Service that provided healthcare for the whole population. New homes were eventually built, and schools provided free secondary education for all. Industry recovered and civilians enjoyed peace and greater prosperity.

Glossary

Air raid Attack by aircraft that drop bombs.

ARP (Air Raid Precautions) This organisation consisted of civilians. It helped people on the home front before and during air raids.

Allotments Small areas of land used for growing fruit or vegetables by individuals.

Anderson shelter Outdoor shelter that could be put up in the garden.

Billeting Making families or households provide a home for evacuees. Billeting officers organised billets.

Blackout Switching off or concealing all lights, particularly in cities, as a precaution against air raids.

Blitz German bombing of British cities. It lasted from September 1940 to May 1941.

Churchill, Winston British prime minister from 1940 to 1945.

Civilians An ordinary member of the public. Not a soldier or a member of any other armed forces.

Conscription Legally calling people to join the services, or do war work.

Evacuate To move people away from a dangerous place.

Evacuee A person who is moved from a dangerous place.

First World War (1914–18) Also called the 'Great War'. Fought between Britain, France, Italy, Russia and the USA (the Allies) and Germany, Austria-Hungary and Turkey (the Central Powers).

GI Nickname for an American soldier. Stands for Government Issue because American soldiers received Government Issue clothing and equipment.

Incendiary bomb A bomb that catches fire when it lands.

Morrison shelter A bomb shelter that could be put up in the home. Consisted of an iron frame and cover.

Munitions Weapons.

Nazi Short for National Socialist. This was an extreme right-wing political party led by Adolf Hitler. It controlled Germany before and during the Second World War.

Rations A fixed amount of something, like food or petrol.

Reserved occupations Jobs essential to the war effort, such as mining, the merchant navy or working on the docks.

Second World War (1939–45) Fought between Nazi Germany, Italy and Japan, (the Axis Powers), and Britain, Commonwealth countries, France, Russia and the USA, known as the Allied Powers.

V1 bomb Flying bombs or rockets launched by Germany against Britain.

Women's Land Army (WLA) Organisation of women who worked on the land.

Further information

Books

My Second World War, Daniel James, Franklin Watts in association with the Imperial War Museum, 2008

Posters and Propaganda in Wartime, Daniel James and Ruth Thomson, Franklin Watts in association with the Imperial War Museum, 2007

World War Two: The Home Front, Ann Kramer, Franklin Watts, 2006

Growing Up in World War Two, Catherine Burch, Franklin Watts, 2005, 2009

The Second World War, Dennis Hamley, Franklin Watts, 2004, 2007

Some useful websites

http://www.iwm.org.uk
The Imperial War Museum's official website, packed with information and photographs.

http://www.bbc.co.uk/history/ww2children/index.shtml
Children of World War Two (1939–45). BBC interactive website. Includes letters from evacuees, information about rationing and what a wartime home was like.

http://www.snaithprimary.eril.net/wcontent.htm
The Home Front: interactive website where you can learn about people's lives during the Second World War and listen to wartime songs.

Note to parents and teachers:
Every effort has been made by the Publishers to ensure that the websites in this book are suitable for children, that they are of the highest educational value, and that they contain no inappropriate or offensive material. However, because of the nature of the Internet, it is impossible to guarantee that the contents of these sites will not be altered. We strongly advise that Internet access is supervised by a responsible adult.

Index